How To Quell Social Anxiety

TO ELIMINATE STRESS ANXIETY FROM YOUR LIFE

Dr. James Stephen

Contents

Introduction

Social anxiety problem is an extreme, tenacious feeling of dread toward being watched and decided by others. This dread can influence work, school, and other day to day exercises. It could actually make it hard to make and keep companions. The uplifting news is social uneasiness problem is treatable. social uneasiness is more than timidity. A trepidation doesn't disappear and influences regular exercises, fearlessness, connections and work or school life. Many individuals every so often stress over friendly circumstances, yet somebody with social uneasiness feels excessively stressed previously, during and after them.

Stress is surprisingly risky, as a matter of fact. You've presumably heard that it can raise your pulse, improving the probability of a stroke in the far off future, however as of late a medical coverage pamphlet guaranteed that 90% of visits to an essential consideration specialist were pressure related messes. Furthermore, stress frequently makes individuals respond in unfortunate ways, like smoking, drinking liquor, eating ineffectively, or turning out to be truly dormant. This harms the body, notwithstanding the mileage of stress itself.

We feel strain to do these things since we assume we HAVE, not on the grounds that we WANT to. It is frequently challenging for individuals to simply say "No". Not saying that little word develops pointless assumptions and commitments that make us restless. We will all go through circumstances that can cause us to feel worried or restless. The reasons are numerous to pay special attention to, however they can incorporate purchasing a property, remaining with visitors (parents in law!), harassing, tests, dealing with kids, overseeing funds, relationship issues, voyaging, and so on.

Anxiety or Stress

As opposed to mainstream thinking, there is a contrast among pressure and tension. Stress comes from the tensions we feel throughout everyday life, as we are moved around by work or whatever other undertaking that overwhelms our psyches and bodies, adrenaline is delivered, delayed stay of the chemical causes gloom, expanded circulatory strain and different changes and adverse consequences. One of these adverse consequences is nervousness. With tension, dread defeats all feelings joined by stress and trepidation, making the individual a hermit and an apprehensive sack. Different side effects are chest agony, dazedness and windedness, and fits of anxiety.

Stress is brought about by a current pressure causing variable or stressor. Tension is pressure that go on after that stressor passes. Stress can emerge from any circumstance or believed that causes you to feel disappointed, furious, apprehensive, or even restless. What is unpleasant for one individual isn't really distressing for another. Nervousness is a sensation of trepidation or dread and is quite often joined by sensations of looming destruction. The wellspring of this disquiet isn't generally known or perceived, which can add to the trouble you feel.

Stress is the manner in which our bodies and brains respond to something that disturbs our typical equilibrium throughout everyday life; an illustration of stress is the response we feel when we are terrified or compromised. During distressing occasions, our adrenal organs discharge adrenaline, a chemical that initiates our body's guard systems, making our hearts pound, circulatory strain to rise, muscles to tense and the students of our eyes to expand. As indicated by the Anxiety and Depression Association of America, Social tension is the apprehension about being judged and assessed adversely by others, prompting deep-seated insecurities, mediocrity, shame, embarrassment, and sadness. Notice that the definition says social nervousness prompts sentiments shame and embarrassment, it's amusing looking at this logically. At the point when we experience social nervousness, we fear getting humiliated; however in all actuality, a large portion of the shame we feel is from our social uneasiness as a matter of fact, individuals with social tension are probably not going to encounter many humiliating minutes, since they are keen.

The embarrassment brought about by friendly nervousness, is embarrassment that did not depend on genuine input, however simply on pessimistic considerations and feelings, this is far more terrible than the genuine embarrassment experienced from giving a terrible show or being dismissed for a date. How do I have any idea about this? I've encountered both social nervousness and genuine embarrassment (ordinarily), and despite the fact that i've been dismissed by numerous ladies and i've given some incredibly abnormal class introductions, the genuine aggravation i've encountered isn't from humiliating minutes like that, the genuine torment was from the dangers I didn't take, from the steady distress of social uneasiness.

This implies that childless ladies may not encounter pressure to similar recurrence or degree as ladies with kids. This intends that for ladies with youngsters, it is especially essential to set aside a few minutes for yourself; you will be in a superior mood to help your children and face the everyday test of being a parent once your anxiety is diminished.

Anxiety, then again, is a sensation of disquiet. Everybody encounters this when confronted with a distressing circumstance, for instance before a test or interview, or during a time of stress like a disease. It's generally expected to feel restless while confronting something troublesome or risky and gentle nervousness can be a good and supportive experience.

The Five Models

There are presently five logical models which make sense of how nervousness creates and works. It isn't so one of these models is right, fairly, every one of these models complete one another.

Cognizance is just an extravagant word for thought. Considerations can set off tension, envision you are driving on the thruway and you start to consider getting in an auto collision, you envision letting completely go, crushing into another vehicle, and you see yourself creeping out of the destruction, scarcely alive. These contemplations lead to additional comparable considerations, and your feelings start to match your reasoning. You begin to feel awkward, your pulse expands, your muscles worry, your breathing becomes whimsical. Everything began with your negative contemplations.

This thought process isn't new, even the Buddha said that we are a result of our reasoning, in any case, the mental model has as of late become acknowledged in established researchers. As a matter of fact, CBT, or mental social treatment, is as of now one of the most broadly rehearsed types of treatment in view of how successful the mental strategy is.

The mental model makes sense of how our tensions winding crazy. We have a pessimistic thought, such as being embarrassed for asking or pound out on the town, then; at that point, we feel restless feelings because of these contemplations. These restless feelings feel so terrible that we become involved with contemplating the apparent future embarrassment more, which creates more restless feelings, etc. The mental model demonstrates the way that tension can be a pessimistic criticism circle: pessimistic idea prompts restless feeling which prompts more pessimistic considerations, and so on.

How might you transform your perspective? We'll cover this in broad detail soon. Before that, we should take a gander at the secret inclination model.

The secret inclination model expresses that nervousness is brought about by a feeling of dread toward gloomy feelings. This thought came about in light of the fact that it was seen that individuals with nervousness are practically all staggeringly pleasant. Assuming that you have social tension, odds are you don't begin contentions and supervisor individuals around on an everyday premise, all things considered, you treat everyone around you well, too well as a matter of fact. At the point when individuals are disturbing you, you presumably don't manage that contention straightforwardly and decisively, you likely remain quiet about those feelings.

Obviously, this had outcomes, rather than going through a time of profound (and normal) trouble, I encountered something undeniably more excruciating. A while after my dad's passing; I had my most memorable fit of anxiety. One evening, I was playing drums when I saw an unusual aggravation and deadness in my left arm. The idea entered my thoughts, "Can't torment in my left arm mean I'm having a coronary failure?" however I disregarded this idea. A few minutes after the fact, the sentiments strengthened, and my heart began hustling, I felt unsteady, and I even felt like I was going to black out. I couldn't resist the opportunity to feel that something truly horrible was going to occur. I continued figuring I may be having a coronary failure. I would have rather not thought this, however the end continued to come up, once more, and once more, and once more. This formed into an out and outfit of anxiety that went on for a few hours, for the entire length, I felt like I was biting the dust.

Afterward, these curbed feelings surface as tension. Feelings are intended to be communicated, and when we totally shut them out, they track down one more method for showing themselves. As per the secret inclination model, when you really express the feelings that you have been clutching, your nervousness will vanish.

I encountered this since feelings can't be disregarded. Overlooking compelling feelings, particularly, has critical results. These sentiments will discover a smart method for surfacing, and on the off chance that you don't allow this to happen normally, this can without much of a stretch transform into tension. At the point when you have social tension, you figure out how to hush up about gloomy feelings. In the event that you're disappointed with somebody, you remain quiet about it, assuming you have eyes for somebody; you hush up about it, assuming you get a handle on left, you hush up about it.

Aversion is the reason for all nervousness. At the point when you fear something, you begin to keep away from it. Assuming you fear making new companions, for instance, you try not to go out or drawing in with outsiders. This aversion makes a rising pressure towards the activity you're keeping away from. The more you stay away from it, the more restless you get towards it. The more you try not to converse with outsiders, the more you become scared of it. As this gathers speed over months or even years, the evasion makes horrendous degrees of tension so extreme that gathering new individuals appears to be a capital punishment. Despite the fact that, unabashedly, it's anything but no joking matter by any means.

To really liberate yourself from your tensions, you should open yourself to what you dread. Assuming that you're anxious about levels, you should deliberately set off that nervousness by placing yourself in a high spot. Assuming you're apprehensive about open talking, you should give discourses to beat that dread really. Assuming you're anxious about asking you're pound out on the town, that tension won't disappear until you ask them out.

Uneasiness is unreasonable, when you deal with your nerves directly; you will understand that the adverse results you envisioned were a figment of your imagination. At the point when you give a discourse, the group won't boo you and giggle at you, when you ask your crush out, they will not embarrass you, sure, they could dismiss you, yet they won't attempt to hurt you.

This book is going location social uneasiness from the perspective of these three models. We will utilize experimentally approved techniques to take a savvy, bit by bit way to deal with beating your uneasiness. Nervousness can feel like an unconquerable adversary that causes you interminable and pointless misery, however uneasiness can be vanquished and this interaction begins today.

Assume Liability

I had encountered quite a while of devastating social tension, was that something can be survived. We are instructed that mental issues, similar to uneasiness and melancholy are made by imbalanced cerebrum science. However, current examination doesn't back up this case.

Any of us with tension and misery are directed to feel like casualties; our cerebrum science is imbalanced and we're told just a pill can fix it. On the off chance that the pill doesn't work, we're in a tough situation. The possibility that we are the casualties of a sickness that is beyond our reach suggests that our tension and sadness isn't our shortcoming, which is, in numerous ways, valid, yet it likewise suggests that we are casualty to a cerebrum that isn't working accurately, and this is deceiving.

Investigations discovered that antidepressants further develop misery (and uneasiness), so researchers were directed to the end that conditions like nervousness were brought about by a synthetic irregularity in the mind, an unevenness that could be fixed with the right medication.

However great as the rationale that says despondency and nervousness may be brought about by a substance irregularity in the cerebrum looks on paper, many years of later logical examination have driven the end to appear to be old, and glaringly misrepresentative of reality.

I need to make sense of why it's significant. In the event that a compound unevenness is prompting your social uneasiness, the most ideal way to further develop it is to consume medications that will change your cerebrum science. The substance lopsidedness would not have anything to do with your everyday considerations and ways of behaving, thus you would be a casualty to your failing mind. This would mean it's not your issue, and that it's additionally not your obligation to move along.

I don't say this softly, on the grounds that I for one comprehend how difficult social nervousness can be: social tension beginnings and closures with your viewpoints and ways of behaving, the two of which, you can change.

My nervousness arrived at its pinnacle not long after the unexpected demise of my dad, I was unable to adapt to this, so I created uneasiness, and afterward in light of the fact that I created tension, my cerebrum science became imbalanced.

Incalculable examinations have shown that lead changes can change mind science. In one survey, a phony treatment drug coordinated to Parkinson's patients changed part's dopamine levels1. In another study2, Harvard specialist, Amy Cuddy found that taking on a power present for only 2 minutes will grow your testosterone levels (strength compound) by around 20% and decline your cortisol levels by around 20%. Various assessments found that when people experience a change of status, their serotonin levels change considering this (this is an immediate consequence of the prevalent approaches to acting that the singular takes on when their status increases). Focuses on like these show that direct changes frontal cortex science, suggesting that the disorder hypothesis which communicates that: anxiety is a result of an engineered imbalance in the psyche, is completely misguided. Imbalanced psyche manufactured substances don't cause strain, when you have apprehension, your frontal cortex engineered materials change a brief time frame later. This proposes that strain is achieved by something through and through insignificant to mind science.

What's the importance here? That lead changes are practical for treating social pressure. Actually, social plans have been seen as in some action as fruitful as medications for treating strain and depression3. Alter your approach to acting, and your brain science will change in this way.

I was unable to try and ask a young lady out on the town, in eleventh grade my crush inclined in to kiss me at a party, I was restless to such an extent that I in a real sense evaded her kiss and left her and afterward left the party. I didn't address her again for a really long time.

A significant number of these strategies were enchantment pill type arrangements, similar to the profound opportunity method which comprises of tapping on your 'meridians' while saying the expression, "Despite the fact that I have this nervousness, I love and acknowledge myself." Unfortunately, none of the sorcery pill arrangements worked; there was no simple to-process handy solution for social tension.

Quiet Down With Visualization

The motivation behind perception is to permit you to rapidly kill mental pressure, strain, and restless reasoning. Perception can be utilized when you feel focused on and is especially useful when your brain is agitating with contemplations of dread and tension.

There is no set in stone manner to play out the representation. Be natural with it and don't feel like you'll not be able to make it happen on the off chance that you feel like you're not truly adept at seeing mental pictures. However long your consideration is on the activity, you will get benefits.

This representation cycle, when rehearsed as often as possible, is extremely viable in dispensing with well established mental nerves or meddlesome contemplations. For most extreme advantage, exercise ought to be performed for longer than 10 minutes all at once, as anything more limited won't yield recognizable outcomes.

Sitting or standing, shut your eyes and concentrate on your breath. To become mindful of your breathing, put one hand on your upper chest and the other on your paunch. Take in and let your stomach grow forward as you breathe in and delicately move back as you breathe out. Continuously inhale with a similar profundity and attempt to keep a consistent musicality.

Your hand on your chest ought to have next to zero development. Once more, attempt to take in a similar profundity each time you breathe in. This is called Diaphragmatic Breathing.

At the point when you feel OK with this procedure, attempt to slow your breathing rate by establishing a brief delay subsequent to breathing out and prior to breathing in once more. At first, it might feel like you're not getting sufficient air, but rather with customary practice, this more slow speed will before long begin to feel great.

Presently move your thoughtfulness regarding your feet. Attempt to feel your feet, as a matter of fact. Check whether you can feel each toe. Envision the foundation of your feet and imagine roots gradually developing through your bottoms and down into the earth. The roots are developing at a sped up rate and venturing profound into the dirt of the earth. You are currently solidly established in the earth and feel stable like an extraordinary oak or redwood.

Hold that feeling of grounded security and insurance for a couple of seconds. Whenever you have made an overwhelming inclination or impression of being grounded like a tree, imagine a haze of brilliant light framing high above you. A pillar from the radiant cloud raises a ruckus around town of your head and touches off a dash of splendid white light that gradually dives from your head down your whole body, legs, and toes.

By envisioning the various circumstances, you are permitting your brain to free itself. It resembles making an impression on your mind that when you shut your eyes and begin this interaction, now is the ideal time to relinquish all that you were intellectually sticking to, including restless reasoning.

Many individuals don't do these representations in their room, however in another room prior to hitting the sack. Like that, when they go into the room and close the entryway, they are abandoning mental pressure and restless reasoning. Simply ensure you have the valuable chance to zero in on your psychological pictures completely.

Representation as a device for managing mental pressure is exceptionally successful. In the event that this representation is done appropriately, you can accomplish a profound feeling of internal quiet. This method likely won't attempt to assist with finishing a mental breakdown; however it can help that assault all along. It is an exceptionally strong help device to dispose of sensations of tension overall.

Social Media use and Social Anxiety

The new pattern of expanding paces of social uneasiness connects with our rising mechanical access. From the outset, this might appear to be erratic, what could cell phone use and fast web have to do with our condition?

The issue isn't that there's anything inherently terrible about web use, however that web use can become habit-forming. As a matter of fact, web use jumble has proactively been proposed to become genuine condition by established researchers. Web use can make the cerebrum actuate in manners that are alarmingly like that of medication usage4. At the point when individuals with web use jumble utilize the web, region of their mind that are related with fixation actuate.

You may be thinking, so what? Regardless of whether I am dependent on the web, this has nothing to do with social nervousness. It really does, in light of the fact that habit-forming ways of behaving are likewise adapting ways of behaving, they permit you to numb yourself from your pressure, and they are a type of idealism. At the point when you take a gander at your cell phone, you can move away from your genuine issues briefly, yet keeping away from your certifiable pressure doesn't dispose of it.

Web-based Entertainment, Face book likes discharge dopamine very much like a gaming machines and cocaine do. The web major areas of strength for causes of dopamine for a comparative motivation to betting the prizes are variation. This implies that the prizes can't be known ahead of time, when you bet, anticipating the outcome is incomprehensible. At the point when you take a gander at your email, you are don't know whether you will find something invigorating, the equivalent is valid at whatever point you get a notice for a message, or when you take a gander at your Face book page. You could have new likes on your Face book post from prior, and this chance is energizing, the dubious chance that the web will prompt compensating occasions like this makes it so habit-forming.

You may be thinking, so what? Regardless of whether I am dependent on the web, this has nothing to do with social uneasiness. It really does, in light of the fact that habit-forming ways of behaving are likewise adapting ways of behaving, they permit you to numb yourself from your pressure, and they are a type of idealism. At the point when you take a gander at your cell phone, you can move away from your certifiable issues briefly, however staying away from your true pressure doesn't dispose of it.

Sadly, you have consistent admittance to adapting to your pressure by means of cell phone. Social tension isn't brought about by web fixation, yet it is sustained by it5. Our steady admittance to the web permits us to try not to manage our feelings, at whatever point we feel awkward, we take out our telephone and use it to numb ourselves from that uneasiness. This propensity for staying away from our pressure and uneasiness exacerbates our nervousness: rather than adapting to our tension normally, we generally have an enchanted pill in our pocket that gives us a break.

Feeling awkward is absolutely normal, these sentiments are your body's approach to letting you know that you want to make a specific move. Stress and uneasiness highlight genuine north. Assuming you have a restless outlook on conversing with a charming young lady, for instance, it implies that you truly need to meet her. These awkward sentiments are suggestions to take action, and they're unfathomably useful, but since these sentiments are awkward, keeping away from them is simple. Cell phones have made a definitive survival strategy, since we continually approach, and we can reliably keep away from any awkward sentiments, and subsequently abstain from making the fundamental moves to scattering those sentiments.

Manage Stress

As we said, stress is essential for life. There's no avoiding it. Some pressure is great pressure, truth is told. You may not completely accept that this, yet at times pressure can propel us to do things we regularly don't do when loose. Stress can make us adequately fearless to proceed when we would typically falter.

Perceiving the side effects of pressure can be a positive impact as we are constrained to act - and the sooner the better. It's not generally simple to observe why you have pressure in each circumstance, however probably the most well-known occasions that trigger these feelings are the demise of a friend or family member, the introduction of a kid, task advancement, or another relationship. We feel pressure as we correct our lives.

We should be strong to manage pressure actually and assist it with working on our lives, as opposed to controlling it. How would you become solid and tough? Figuring out how to assume command over your pressure and make it works FOR you rather than AGAINST you.

You can likewise concoct your own pressure the executive's tips. The fundamental thought is to recognize the reason for worry and get of it briefly and afterward manage it. Going for a short stroll and noticing objects in nature is another calming. Drinking a glass of water or playing little games are straightforward pressure the executive's procedures. The entire thought is to move your concentration and when you return to the issue, it will not be pretty much as tremendous as it used to be.

Five Speedy Advances

1.   Don't simply stay there. To move! As indicated by numerous analysts, development makes feeling. You might find that when you are inactive, it is more straightforward to become discouraged. Your pulse eases back, less oxygen goes to your cerebrum, and you're drooped some place in a seat, impeding air from arriving at your lungs.

I challenge you now, paying little heed to how you're feeling, to get up and stroll at a lively speed. Perhaps you need to go to an unfilled room and bounce all over a little. It might sound senseless, yet the proof is in the pudding. Attempt it now for a couple of moments. It works like sorcery.

2.   Help others to manage their concerns. It's exceptionally restorative

when you commit yourself to helping other people. You will be astounded to perceive the number of individuals' concerns that are more awful than the ones you might confront. You can offer help to others in various ways. Try not to twist up in bed and let misery and stress assumes control over you.

Go out and help somebody. Be that as it may, watch out. Try not to engage in others' concerns trying to forget your own.

I'm continually called by loved ones when they need to vent or request counsel. I joke and tell them "Don't call the individual 'insane' for exhortation!" But there are times when I stress over the people who call me and I become involved with what they're going through. It simply gives me more pressure than I as of now am and I assume I need to step back and reconsider myself and my needs.

3.   Smell the roses. How would you smell roses? What about putting away a cash to go on that outing you've generally longed for? Visit a country with numerous extraordinary spots to start your creative mind and flash your innovativeness. You really want to detach from your regular day to day existence and adventure out a bit.

4.   Laugh a bit. You've heard that giggling is a decent interior medication. Eases pressure and loosens up muscles. It makes blood stream to the heart and mind. In particular, giggling discharges a compound that frees the group of torment.

Consistently, specialists find new advantages of giggling. Allow me to pose you this inquiry: "Could you at any point utilize a decent portion of gut beating chuckling sometimes?" obviously you can. What are you sitting tight for? Go to a parody club or lease a few interesting motion pictures.

5.   Wear your knees. On the off chance that there was one reasonable cure I could offer you while the going got extreme, it would be petition. Many individuals, contingent upon their confidence, could call this reflection. It doesn't make any difference to me what you call it, as long as you have some place to run.

Money Saving Advantage Examination

You can involve the above segment for some direction assuming you experience difficulty considering what the advantages of social tension are for you. The initial step is to make a rundown of the multitude of advantages of social nervousness. What is it permitting you to feel (or not feel) and do (or not do), that gives you an advantage of some sort? List at least, three advantages that your social uneasiness is giving you.

Whenever you have finished your rundown of advantages, begin a rundown of expenses. What agony is social nervousness causing you? What is social tension keeping you from encountering? What valuable open doors do you miss consistently in view of your social uneasiness? Once more, list at least, three expenses for social tension.

Then, give each the expenses and advantages an all out weight, amounting to 100. Assuming the expenses are weighed at 70, the advantages would be weighed at 30. This permits you to get some explanation with regards to regardless of whether the expenses of your social tension are valuable.

For additional direction, you can investigate this illustration of money saving advantage examination for social nervousness.

Advantages Of My Social Uneasiness

1.   It keeps me from getting dismissed. I blame social tension so as to keep silent and keep away from social dangers, subsequently; I keep away from the potential for social dismissal.

2.   It permits me to feel like my terrible public activity isn't my issue. By blaming my nervousness, I try not to get a sense of ownership with my public activity.

3.   Social tension gives me a reason to depend on liquor in friendly circumstances. I realize drinking is a truly negative behavior pattern, but since I feel awkward except if I drink, I routinely hit the booze hard in friendly circumstances. If I somehow managed to get a sense of ownership with my public activity, I

wouldn't have a reason to numb myself through drinking.

Expenses Of Social Nervousness

1.   I feel like I'm a detainee as far as I could tell. I don't say a great deal of the things I need to say or begin the discussions I need to begin since I'm apprehensive about a few envisioned outcomes. I feel like I'm continually at battle with myself, and I don't feel better in my own skin along these lines.

2.   Social uneasiness gives me a reason to invest my energy at home alone playing on the web computer games rather than really captivating with others. I'm dependent on these games now and I don't for even a moment appreciate them much.

3.   I'm eighteen and I've never had a sweetheart, social uneasiness has been my reason to try not to confront dismissal from a young lady I like.

In the event that the heaviness of the advantages for social nervousness emerge as more huge than the expenses of social tension, perhaps you ought to quit perusing here in light of the fact that your uneasiness is helping you. Perhaps, however, you should reconsider the loads, since, supposing that the social uneasiness wasn't extraordinarily excruciating; you likely wouldn't peruse a book about how to defeat it.

In the accompanying segment, you will be given a progression of difficulties in view of a helpful method called steady openness. Openness treatment depends on the possibility that the main way out, is through. You can't sneak around your tensions and hope to genuinely conquer them; on the off chance that you're anxious about bugs, grasping a tarantula is the best course to beat your trepidation.

Openness treatment is by definition troublesome, nonetheless, the torment of going through your trepidation endures just for a couple of seconds, though the torment of living in response to that dread is steady and weakening. Whenever you've confronted your feelings of trepidation, they're not all that awful; however on the off chance that you don't confront them, they are continuously affecting you.

The series of difficulties in the following area will expect you to leave your usual range of familiarity so you can discredit your social uneasiness. You will do things that seem like they might get you judged, that seem like they will have significant results. In any case, as you do these difficulties, it will turn out to be certain that those results were a deception.

Only openness isn't sufficient. Tension is self-supporting, and it is feasible to see what happens when you overcome your apprehensions as additional proof that you ought to feel restless. To guarantee this doesn't occur we will utilize demonstrated journaling procedures to take an objective focal point towards what occurs during these difficulties. In your diary, you will be compelled to uncover the nonsensical reasoning causing your nerves, as you compose this diary, you will see that your feelings of dread are as a matter of fact, very ridiculous. You will not have the option to get away from the way that your uneasiness isn't intelligent, and this mindfulness will permit you to relinquish it.

Say "No"

A major issue individuals who are excessively worried have is the capacity to say "No" as needs be. Perhaps your mother maintains that you should accept Grandma to the market, yet you're in a major work project. Perhaps your closest companion inquires as to whether you'd mind dealing with her children when she's made arrangements with you to get a hair style.

There is not a great explanation to say "OK" to everybody. You frequently need to turn them down, as a matter of fact. Assuming that you consent to do things when you truly don't have any desire to, you will kindly individuals. By and large, this is definitely not a terrible quality, yet it very well may be a significant stressor.

Continually attempting to satisfy others is depleting, and numerous wonderful individuals feel restless, stressed, miserable, and tired more often than not. They may not comprehend the reason why nobody does anything for them when they accomplish such a great deal for other people, yet they frequently don't request what they need.

This is the snare I fell into. I generally wound up consenting to accomplish for other people, however when I wanted these equivalent individuals to help me, they were inquisitively occupied.

Individuals who like to if it's not too much trouble, individuals might trust that assuming you ask somebody for help and that individual concurs, that individual is giving it out of commitment, not on the grounds that they truly need to. The idea goes - to help, they would have presented without my inquiring.

At the point when they pause for a minute for themselves, they feel narrow minded, liberal, and blameworthy, which is the reason they are frequently

Go, hurrying to finish things. Since human satisfying individuals achieve a ton and are not difficult to coexist with, they are much of the time the first to be approached to get things done — they are defenseless against being exploited.

I figured out how to figure out how to escape that cycle. You can do exactly the same thing in the event that you see yourself in the portrayal above. Would you like to know how? It's simpler than you naturally suspect!

To begin with, work on saying NO. This is a vital word! Say exactly that as you can, just to hear the word emerge from your mouth. Let's assume it without holding back when you're distant from everyone else. Practice NO expressions like "No, I can't do that" or "No, I would rather not go there." Experiment with straightforward things first and afterward continues on toward additional tough spots.

Quit saying OK constantly. Attempt to delay or calmly inhale prior to answering somebody's solicitation. You might need to answer demands with "I want to ponder this first.

Enjoy short reprieves, regardless of whether you feel regretful. You will not necessarily in all cases feel remorseful, yet you most likely will from the beginning. Recall that your emotional well-being is definitely worth the problem you might need to get from others. The significant thing is you. At the point when you are sound, individuals around you will be as well!

Figure out what satisfies you. For instance, you could appreciate understanding magazines, watching recordings, going to a recreation area, or paying attention to music. Allow you to do these things and afterward appreciate them.

The Journal

After every one of the accompanying difficulties, you will be approached to compose a diary section in which you root out restless and negative reasoning. You will be approached to recognize any bad contemplation that went through your brain while you were participating in the test. Then, at that point, you will recognize why those contemplations are silly. When you know why the considerations are, as a matter of fact, silly, your consciousness of this permits you to relinquish them.

There are eleven mental contortions which can variety your reasoning when you are encountering uneasiness, before every diary passage, you will be given a rundown of these twists, nonetheless, go ahead and focus on this segment in the event that you can't recall what any of them mean.

1. Go big or go home thinking: You feel that not exclusively will she reject you, however you will constantly be dismissed, you will bomb as well as you are a disappointment. You could see yourself as very off-kilter personally, another person may know that they've had abnormal minutes, yet you consider yourself to be off-kilter in a high contrast way. So obviously, you shouldn't converse with her, you're off-kilter, and thusly, regardless of anything, so will your discussion with her be.

2. Overgeneralization: You imagine that in light of the fact that your crush dismissed you once, that you will continuously be dismissed. You imagine that since when you attempted to champion yourself your folks hollered at you, you can never advocate for yourself without this backfire. You don't consider what is happening is unique, every individual is unique, and that you will act distinctively at various times.

3. Mental Filter: You have a negative supposition that colors everything adversely. You feel that somebody may be unkind to you, and the sum total of your views go to the potential manners by which they may be spiteful to you as opposed to monitoring the a wide range of conceivable outcomes.

4. Limiting the Positive: You don't see the positive prospects, maybe you will have a decent discussion, maybe you will get that advancement assuming you request, yet you disregard these conceivable outcomes and focus on the negative other options.

5. Fortune-telling: You envision a negative future. You think as though something negative will undoubtedly occur, as though you are a spiritualist, however your feelings of dread aren't founded on realities.

6. Mind-Reading: You could believe that when you make a joke everybody will giggle at you and embarrass you for your disgraceful endeavor, you're thinking as though you can determine what individuals are thinking, yet you can't.

6. Close to home thinking: You feel restless, so you justify that something awful should be going to occur. Rather than contemplating the potential results in a consistent way, your feelings make you reach ridiculous determinations.

7. Amplification and Minimization: You make mountains out of molehills; you think there are extreme results that don't actually exist. On the off chance that your crush rejects you, you could figure she will slap you, or will giggle at you and you will be made into a social outsider, obviously, this won't ever occur. You can likewise limit your positive characteristics, and persuade yourself they don't actually exist.

8. Should explanations: You add force to your tension by letting yourself know you 'shouldn't feel restless. You are letting yourself know that your pessimistic feelings are off-base, and by marking them as off-base, you are making them more impressive than they unabashedly are.

9. Naming: This is outrageous overgeneralization, assuming you were snickered immediately for a humiliating second, you don't see it as a humiliating second, you see it as evidence that you are an abnormal individual overall. On the off chance that you gave a terrible show in school you don't see it as a terrible show, you consider yourself to be an awful moderator.

10. Fault: You can fault yourself or fault others. At the point when you fault yourself, you beat yourself up over a little error and make a huge deal about it providing it with a ton of close to home

power. At the point when you fault others, you remove the obligation from yourself, "My folks let me play computer games the entire day as opposed to associating with others, and it's their shortcoming." Or, "since I attempted weed I've been unique, presently I can't feel good around others." Blame allows you to feel like a casualty, and to catastrophist your concerns, subsequently liberating you of obligation.

Offer A Reprieve

Frequently, we know inside ourselves that we want a break. That break can be a finished excursion or an end of the week escape. One way or the other, breaking out of the monotonous routine can be staggeringly liberating and an extraordinary method for disposing of pressure and tension.

Sadly, many individuals figure they can't stand to sit around idly. This is poisonous reasoning. Get out and go!

How often have you continued functioning, realizing that you are not committing yourself 100 percent to the job needing to be done? How often have you perused or composed a similar sentence again and again, while your brain is meandering and pondering different things? How frequently have you needed to have some time off from your family or children, yet dreaded the results of doing as such? Now is the ideal time to have some time off!

For what reason don't we permit ourselves a 'break'? Maybe we feel that we don't merit it or that there is basically an excessive amount to be finished. There are numerous certified purposes behind expecting to get done with tasks and undertakings; be that as it may, we may likewise incidentally have 'stowed away plans' concerning why we can't stop for a break.

It very well may be self image. Certain individuals very much prefer to boast about 'how late they needed to attempt to finish an undertaking' or 'how much exertion they put in to take care of business so rapidly'. This sort of individual frequently tries to dazzle others with their endeavors, consequently lifting their confidence all the while.

Perhaps you assume you can't enjoy some time off. "I cannot stop; I simply need to complete this." Does this sound recognizable? "I can't stop in light of the fact that the work must be finished, WHY? So I can go directly to the following thing, and the following, and the following, etc..." This individual will observe that there is continuously something that must be finished, which will continually keep you from having some time off.

Dispose of that idea! You can get a few astounding advantages by simply carving out a little margin for yourself! Permitting your psyche or potentially body to rest can assist with concentrating; hone your knowledge, and increment inspiration. Furthermore, getting some much needed rest eases pressure, can help with the recuperation of tired muscles, and furthermore advances the revelation that life is something beyond working.

So you've concluded that a break is fundamental. Bravo! A break can be anything from a 10-minute contemplation meeting to an outing all over the planet, and in the middle between. I figure a break ought to be something that takes your brain off the monotony of daily existence.

So contingent upon how long you need to unwind, you could appreciate perusing, watching a film, cooking, playing with the children, riding a bike or driving, practicing or playing sports, voyaging or simply resting!

While you rest, most importantly, give yourself an opportunity to make it happen and don't feel remorseful about it. You will acquire a great deal from this spare energy, so partake in the time you are giving yourself.

Life will happen without you, and as opposed to everything your brain might be saying to you, everybody will get by - in any event, when you're not there! Allow everything to proceed to zero in on you rather than everybody around you!

In the event that you're feeling drained, unmotivated, or simply needing a break, don't be a saint or check out at it with malignance. You may really find that truly having some time off will truly assist you with turning out to be more proficient and compelling in all aspects of your life. Furthermore, you'll get the genuinely necessary re-energize of your "batteries" that you want and merit!

Task One

A Day without Screens

The test:

Go for a whole day without utilizing your cell phone, web, or TV.

Description:

This challenge will show you in an instinctive manner how ward you've become on your cell phone for adapting to day to day pressure. You can expect that this challenge will be very awkward. To succeed, you will most likely need to put your cell phone out of your vision, on the off chance that you have simple admittance to your cell phone; your programmed reaction can undoubtedly dominate. The way that this will be so difficult is characteristic of the way that we are dependent on innovation, and that we've become dependent on it.

Your day without innovation might be disproportionally upsetting, and it would be not difficult to think this is on the grounds that web use is a decent survival technique. However, it's practically the inverse. At the point when you remove a wellspring of a habit, you make a lot of pressure since when you become dependent on something, you become subject to it to ease your pressure. When something is a fixation, this dependence on that enslavement for stress-help keeps you from adapting to the pressure in a sound manner. Enslavement based adapting doesn't kill the wellspring of the pressure, it just numbs you to it for a period; the fundamental pressure is still there, and the more you adapt to it utilizing your dependence, the more regrettable that hidden pressure becomes and the more you depend on your dependence on adapt to it.

As you go during your time without electronic media, notice how you feel. What's more, notice the way that you feel when you get an inclination to utilize your cell phone or your PC. You might find that at whatever point you feel awkward, you get an inclination to adapt to that distress through innovation. If so, a decent sign diminishing your web utilize would be a decent initial step to lessening your social uneasiness as well as your tension and stress overall.

Assuming you limit your admittance to your cell phone, you will not have the option to with such ease keep away from social connection, removing this unfortunate adapting choice will make the choice of really cooperating with individuals significantly more engaging in any event, when you feel restless.

In the event that you find that doing without electronic media for a day is troublesome, it demonstrates that you might acquire a ton of significant worth by going on an electronic media diet. At any rate, this would mean switching off warnings for messages, Face book messages, and so on. Probably, this would mean leaving your cell phone at home as the day progressed, and on the off chance that you truly need to stay in contact with individuals over the course of the day, you could purchase a telephone that doesn't have full web access.

These means might appear to be outrageous, and they might be troublesome, yet the drawn out benefits are worth the effort. Steady admittance to screens permits you to be anyplace yet where you really are, continually keeping away from reality makes reality more distressing, and this makes it more challenging to see the value in the easily overlooked details throughout everyday life. By restricting your admittance to electronic media.

Task Two

Eye To Eye Connection

The test:

Go to a public spot and visually connect with a sum of 5 outsiders until they turn away.

Description:

You can do this test at a bar, a bustling road, the shopping center, your school grounds, or even a bustling store. Visually connecting can feel awkward, from one viewpoint since we fear being judged, and then again in light of the fact that we are anxious about the possibility that that it's too obtrusive, that individuals could do without being checked out. Being excessively circumspect is one of the significant reasons for social nervousness, and discovering that exercises like visually connecting aren't hostile is a significant stage towards beating it.

At the point when you see somebody, give them a couple of moments to return eye to eye connection, and in the event that they don't, turn away (the direct isn't toward simply gaze at individuals). On the off chance that they really do return eye to eye connection, take a gander at them with a slight grin until they turn away. When they turn away, you can turn away too.

This might be testing, and it might require some investment, recollect that the more troublesome this challenge is, the more that you need to acquire from it, assuming it were absolutely simple, it wouldn't have a lot of significant worth. You are figuring out how to open yourself to your social nervousness to demonstrate to yourself that your apprehensions are silly.

Model diary section 3:

1. Go big or go home Thinking.

2. Overgeneralization

3. Mental Filter.

4. Limiting the Positive.

5. Mind-perusing.

6. Fortune-Telling.

7. Amplification and Minimization.

8. Profound thinking

9. Should proclamations

10. Marking.

11. Fault.

Feelings of apprehension:

1. I took a gander at a man strolling by and saw a mean look all over, I was anxious about the possibility that that he planned to stroll towards me and shout at me for being a wet blanket.

Mental Distortions:

This believed is certainly win big or bust, perhaps he was a piece vexed, however he won't approach me and greet me.

I was additionally limiting the positive that I had propelled myself and achieved the test. I was rushing to make the judgment call that he was thinking a specific way or going to act a specific way despite the fact that there was no proof in light of the real world.

I was most certainly amplifying what is happening, letting myself know something embarrassing planned to occur, when it truly wasn't (and didn't).

I was utilizing close to home thinking, I persuaded myself that since I felt restless, it probably implied something terrible was truly going to occur.

Task Three

How About We Go To The Shopping Center!

The test:

Stroll around the shopping center without anyone else (ideally during occupied hours) for something like 30 minutes.

Description:

This could appear to be too simple to ever be a test. Notwithstanding, you wouldn't believe and observe that it is very awkward to go to a region with a lot of individuals all alone. Regardless of whether it ends up being genuinely simple, you can involve this test as an amazing chance to turn out to be more mindful of your inward exchange. Additionally, recall, that difficult yourself an excessive amount of excessively fast can blow up. Analyst Roy Baumeister said that one of the main motivations for the discretion issue is arrogance in one's self discipline. This challenge is a stage towards confronting your social tension, without being an impossible test.

As you stroll around the shopping center, focus on any genuine fears that go through your head, you may be amazed and observe that many exceptionally regrettable contemplations are going through your mind on autopilot. This is great, on the grounds that as we learned, concerns make restless sentiments, by becoming mindful of fears, you can relinquish them and change them. As you do this, your restless sentiments will scatter also.

1. Go big or go home thinking.

2. Overgeneralization

3. Mental Filter.

4. Limiting the Positive.

5. Mind-perusing.

6. Fortune-Telling.

7. Amplification and Minimization.

8. Close to home thinking

9. Should explanations

10. Marking.

Genuine concerns:

 Individuals will believe I'm very odd for strolling around the shopping center without help from anyone else.

Mental Distortions:

This believed is mind perusing since I'm going about as though I can clairvoyantly understand what others are thinking, when obviously, I can't.

This is limiting the positive, since who knows, individuals could think I seem to be a fascinating individual to meet. This believed is most certainly amplifying; individuals don't actually ponder somebody strolling by that amount, if by any means.

I'm likewise naming myself as odd for strolling around the shopping center, instead of marking it as something surprising to do.

I'm suggesting that I shouldn't stroll around the shopping center since individuals will pass judgment on me for it.

I'm suggesting that I shouldn't stroll

Task Four

Occupied Sidewalk

The test:

Go to a public spot with a ton of people walking through, and lie on the ground for 1 moment.

Description:

At the point when you have social tension, you sift through specific activities as unseemly or strange. Contradicting somebody turns out to be inconceivably troublesome in light of the fact that it seems like the strain this makes is a feeling that should be stayed away from. By and large, when you have social tension, you likewise want to fit in, and to abstain from doing whatever surprising that could get you judged. Thus, you channel your words and your activities, continually letting yourself know what you can and can't say. Somewhat of a channel is helpful, there are a few things you shouldn't say or do. In any case, our channels will quite often be undeniably greater than is needed, and we sift through making statements that show our special character, we abstain from saying anything that we think could get us decided as abnormal.

This challenge drives you to accomplish something strange deliberately, to accomplish something that conflicts with business as usual, and it shows that doing something else won't get you judged or embarrassed. As a matter of fact, individuals won't mind much by any means, and on the off chance that they do, they will just need to help you. This is the very thing that my understudy Andrew found when he did this test, he was stunned that not in the least did nobody ridicule him, however that somebody approached him to ensure he was OK (that he hadn't dropped or something like that).

We learn through long stretches of social molding how to fit in. Yet, the pieces of our character are unique, that are unusual, that make us what our identity is. Certifiable self-articulation expects that you become familiar with being a little bizarre, that you let go of the voice in your mind, what top rated creator Jamie Weal calls your inward Woody Allen. This exercise will show you that the outcomes you figure you will look for being abnormal are a figment of your imagination; they're not in view of anything outer.

Model diary section 4 :

1. Go big or go home thinking.

2. Overgeneralization

3. Mental Filter.

4. Limiting the Positive.

5. Mind-perusing.

6. Fortune-Telling.

7. Amplification and Minimization.

8. Close to home thinking

9. Should proclamations

10. Marking.

Anxieties:

1. I believed that as I lay on the walkway, individuals would giggle at me and structure a group. I even felt that security would be called to accompany me out of the shopping center.

Mental Twists:

I was fortune-telling that horrible things would happen despite the fact that I had no proof for these apprehensions.

I was mind-perusing by letting myself that I realized know individuals thinking, I don't think they were really pondering me much by any stretch of the imagination.

I was amplifying the earnestness of the circumstance, believing that it would mix a commotion.

I was utilizing personal thinking, since I felt awkward, I accepted others would feel what I was doing was very peculiar or unseemly.

Task Five

Ask Outsiders For Headings

The test:

Move toward 3 outsiders and ask them for bearings to a close by area (like great food close by).

Description:

A specific degree of tension towards meeting outsiders is entirely normal. Our minds developed over a time of countless years in perilous conditions. Our progenitors lived in little clans of 50-150 individuals, and in the event that they another person, somebody who wasn't from their clan, this could address mortal risk. Anybody unfamiliar could be a foe, they could be from a fighting clan. Our progenitors who aimlessly moved toward outsiders wouldn't pass on their qualities since they would meet an inconvenient destiny because of some risky individual from another clan.

Your cerebrum advanced to be unfortunate of outsiders, in light of the fact that in the climate your mind developed, outsiders were extremely risky. Be that as it may, this dread is presently not applicable, and by trying not to converse with outsiders, this dread will just turn out to be increasingly more made a huge deal about over the long run. Luckily, in spite of the fact that your mind normally fears outsiders, it can likewise be prepared to understand that outsiders are as a matter of fact, not compromising by any stretch of the imagination. By meeting new individuals, you will demonstrate to your mind that outsiders are innocuous, yet at the same generally amicable.

I recollect when my social nervousness was even from a pessimistic standpoint, I expected individuals would treat me selfishly, that individuals would have no desire to meet me, and that assuming I acquainted myself with a more bizarre they would offer me a disturbed look prior to strolling while throwing a mini tantrum. As I constrained myself to overcome my apprehensions and meet new individuals, I discovered that these considerations were totally unreasonable. As I met an ever increasing number of individuals, obviously in addition to the fact that people were not mean, however they were by and large kind and agreeable.

Doing this challenge the most terrible that could happen is somebody could say, "How about you simply take a gander at your cell phone for bearings?" If this occurs, you can say, "Valid statement", or, "I didn't carry my cell phone with me."

Ask the individual you approach something like, "Hello, sorry to interfere, yet do you know anyplace with great food to eat close by?" They might say they can't imagine anything or they might guide you to a specific area, one way or the other, you're demonstrating that any catastrophizing negative contemplations you might have about outsiders are silly.

Model diary section 5:

1. Go big or go home thinking.

2. Overgeneralization

3. Mental Filter.

4. Limiting the Positive.

5. Mind-perusing.

6. Fortune-Telling.

7. Amplification and Minimization.

8. Close to home thinking

9. Should explanations

10. Naming.

11. Fault.

Fears:

I felt that the more abnormal I drew closer would think I was hitting on them and that they would be outraged. I believed that they could blame me for being bizarre or provide me with a look of loathing.

Mental Distortions:

This believed was certainly limiting the positive, the young lady could have been satisfied to meet me.

I was mind-perusing by letting myself know she was considering assortment negative contemplations.

I was fortune telling by foreseeing an adverse result not in view of proof, but rather based restless reasoning.

I was without a doubt amplifying the issue, individuals don't act so decisively as I was envisioning over something so exceptionally commonplace as requesting bearings.

I was thinking through feeling, my gloomy feelings made me believe that something truly pessimistic will undoubtedly occur.

You might be shocked to find that individuals don't pass judgment on you, that generally they will disregard you, and that assuming anybody sees you, they're bound to support you than to peer down at you. Moving out in the open is abnormal, however there's nothing hostile or off-base about it, and any uneasiness this gives you is absolutely silly.

Dance anyway you like, simply remember that you will escape this activity however much you put into it. Assuming you weakly sway your head all over, don't anticipate getting much from this activity, notwithstanding, assuming you drive yourself to hit the dance floor with complete excitement, you will truly grow your usual range of familiarity, and power yourself to understand that your apprehension about being judged and embarrassed is absurd.

For this test, consider making it an everyday propensity, you can move around your area, or even dance en route to work or school. Becoming familiar with being peculiar is very freeing, and powers you to relinquish your mental self view and let go of thinking often such a huge amount about individuals' thought process of you.

While I strolled around wondering whether or not to begin moving, I envisioned that shopping center security would certainly accompany me off the premises. That's what I envisioned assuming I moved openly, individuals would take a gander at me with repugnance and that my standing would be destroyed, I envisioned this news returning to my companions and turning into a social outcast along these lines.

Mutilated thinking:

This believing was win big or bust, that's what I envisioned assuming individuals thought my moving was unusual, that it would turn out to be disastrous to the point that it would for all time ruin my standing.

I was limiting the positive, perhaps individuals would have found my moving engaging, perhaps it would have been a positive entertaining memory for them.

I was mind perusing again by letting myself know that I realized how individuals would respond to my moving. I was fortune telling by making an entire situation that would work out in which my future would be destroyed.

I was significantly amplifying the outcomes to moving openly, envisioning it would destroy as long as I can remember.

I was thinking inwardly, I envisioned adverse results since I felt awful, however I had no real way to realize what might truly occur.

Individuals with social uneasiness will generally have weaknesses in close connections. Dating requires an elevated degree of profound weakness, and you should have the option to face challenges. Regardless of whether you are right now in a close connection, this challenge will be valuable since you will confront your apprehension about dismissal (in the event that you're stressed over what your accomplice could think, inquire as to whether it's OK to do this in advance).

The test is to straightforwardly ask a more unusual you meet out in the open out on the town, you're not to start up a discussion in advance, just straightforwardly ask somebody out on the town. The objective isn't to get an indeed, it's really to get dismissed.

Why? Since you will demonstrate to yourself that dismissal is definitely not no joking matter, it doesn't need to make a difference, and being dismissed surely isn't the apocalypse. This challenge will cause you to understand that in spite of the fact that dismissal is awkward, not something horrendous should be stayed away from no matter what. The dismissal could hurt briefly, however not close to however much you anticipate that it should.

To achieve this test, go to a public spot like a shopping center once more, move toward an outsider, and say the accompanying, "Greetings, I saw you strolling by and thought you were appealing. Might you want to go out on the town with me?" You can express this with various stating assuming you like; the key part is that you should unequivocally ask them for a date.

Anxieties

Before I moved toward the main young lady, I felt that she would holler at me, and that her sweetheart would stroll over and beat me senseless.

Contorted thinking:

This was win big or bust thinking since I envisioned that on the off chance that the young lady didn't say OK, she would dismiss me totally and cruelly.

I was limiting the positive, she could have been complimented that I asked her out, and she could have even said OK (in spite of the fact that she didn't).

I was mind-perusing by envisioning I realized she would see my methodology as hostile and outlandish.

I was fortune-telling by envisioning an entire scene working out in which I was embarrassed.

I was, to the surprise of no one, amplifying the gamble I was taking, persuading myself that I could encounter terrible outcomes.

I was thinking that something horrendous would occur, however this depended on my gloomy feelings, rather than being founded on legitimate proof.

Loosening up At Work

Short breathers aren't the main times you can pause for a minute for yourself. Experience has truly instructed me that espresso (or smoke) breaks can really add to the pressure you feel when you're working.

A portion of the ideas we've given you in this book can positively be rehearsed working, yet tragically, others

You cannot. This is a dependable technique to assist you with unwinding at work.

In the first place, track down a spot to sit. Sit upright, with your back against the rear of the seat, your feet level on the floor and your hands laying gently on your thighs.

If conceivable, shut your eyes. You can do the activity without shutting your eyes, yet shutting them will assist you with loosening up somewhat more. Try not to shut your eyes firmly. Allow your eyelids to hang normally.

Breathe in leisurely through your nose for a count of 5. Pause your breathing for a count of 5. Breathe out leisurely for a count of five. Rehash,

As you tense each arrangement of muscles, do as hard as possible without harming yourself. While delivering the grasp, be basically as loose as could really be expected.

Begin by straining your feet. Do this by pulling your feet off the floor and your toes towards you, keeping your impact points on the floor. Hold for a sluggish count of 5. Discharge pressure. Allow your feet to drop tenderly in reverse. Feel the unwinding.

Ponder how it feels contrasted with when you strained your muscles. Unwind and build up to 5.

Then, at that point, tense your thigh muscles as hard as possible. Hold and build up to 5. Loosen up your muscles and build up to 5.

Contract your abs and hold for a count of 5. Loosen up your muscles and build up to 5. Make certain to sit straight.

Contract your arm and hand muscles, crushing your clench hands as firmly as could really be expected. Hold and build up to 5. Loosen up muscles totally and build up to 5.

Just barely get your upper back by pushing your shoulders back, as though you were attempting to unite your shoulder bones. Hold and build up to 5. Unwind and build up to 5.

Press your shoulders, lifting them toward your ears, as though you were shrugging your shoulders and building up to 5. Unwind and build up to 5.

Contract your neck first by delicately moving your head back (as though taking a gander at the roof) and holding for 5. Unwind for

5. Then, at that point, tenderly lower your head forward and hold for 5. Unwind and build up to 5.

Contract your face muscles. First open your mouth wide and hold for 5. Unwind for 5. Then cause a stir and hold for 5. Unwind for 5. At long last, shut your eyes firmly and hold for 5. Unwind (with eyes delicately shut) for 5.

Finish the activity by relaxing. Breathe in leisurely through your nose for a count of 5. Pause your breathing for a count of 5.

Breathe out leisurely for a count of five. Rehash multiple times. Furthermore, that is all there is to it!

Do this exercise at whatever point you really want to unwind, whether it's on the plane, in the vehicle, or elsewhere you're sitting. As this exercise can be exceptionally unwinding, it ought not to be performed while driving.

Over the long haul, whenever done consistently, this exercise will assist you with perceiving strain in your body. You can loosen up your muscles whenever as opposed to doing the whole activity. Run no less than two times per day for long haul results.

You can foster your own more extended unwinding exercise by adding more muscle gatherings. Recognize your own areas of strain and afterward contract and loosen up that region similarly.

Expand the unwinding advantages of this activity by imagining a quiet scene toward the finish of the activity. Imagine a scene - where you feel loose - exhaustively

For no less than 5 minutes. Recall the cheerful spot? Go there and have a great time!

Watchfulness

In the event that you haven't gained a single thing from perusing this book, we want to believe that you understand and comprehend that THERE IS NO WAY to dispose of pressure from your life totally. What you can do is figure out how to make pressure work FOR you.

Stress the executives isn't quite so troublesome as it might appear. Notwithstanding, we feel compelled to stress this next point as much as possible. Assuming you feel that you have an excessive amount of pressure in your life, it could be useful to converse with your primary care physician, otherworldly advisor, or nearby emotional well-being affiliation. Since stress responses can be a figure gloom, tension, and different issues, they might recommend that you see a specialist, clinician, social laborer, or other qualified guide.

You can hope to feel reduced degrees of social uneasiness, and a level of opportunity that you most likely haven't encountered since you were a kid. In any case, don't anticipate that your social tension should evaporate totally or to disappear until the end of time. Vanquishing social uneasiness takes carefulness, it's a ceaseless interaction. Challenge yourself consistently, and you will change such a lot of that your timid, restless past will appear to be weird and unfamiliar.

You can likewise take a gander at time usage instruments to dispose of a portion of your stressors. At the point when we feel as we need more opportunity to do the things that should be finished, it makes more pressure and can prompt uneasiness that, accept me, you would rather not have!

Assuming any of the difficulties from this book were especially difficult, or were especially gainful, rehash that test for seven days straight to get the most potential worth from it. Doing a test once can assist you with gaining ground, yet doing it on numerous occasions straight will make the close to home examples truly sink in and lead to a lot further change.

Go ahead and concoct your own test, to do, yet it makes you restless: make it happen. Perhaps you've needed to attempt standup satire; perhaps you have needed to share a thing of beauty you made on your web-based entertainment accounts. Anything you've been lingering on, do it now. Utilize the energy you've worked from taking on this book's moves as inspiration to propel yourself considerably further.

In the event that you assume you want assistance, don't hold back. You may not be right 100% of the time. The reason for your pressure might be without reason. In any case, it very well might be physical at its foundations

Since it has become so obvious this, social tension, or any uneasiness, is presently not a reason to get in your own particular manner. You've shown yourself that the psychological jail that was keeping you down and keeping you from genuinely encountering life was a deception. Also, from here onward you can confront your feelings of trepidation with mental fortitude since you realize that the outcomes of doing so are pitiful contrasted with the results of allowing your tension to decide your activities.

Stress is a typical piece of life. In modest quantities, stress is great - it can propel you and assist you with being more useful. In any case, an excess of stress, or a solid pressure reaction, is hurtful.

It can set you up for general medical problems as well as unambiguous physical or mental afflictions like contaminations, coronary illness, or discouragement. Constant, unwavering pressure frequently prompts nervousness and unfortunate ways of behaving like gorging and mishandling liquor or medications.

Similarly as the reasons for pressure differ from one individual to another, what eases pressure isn't something very similar for everybody. As a general rule, nonetheless, making specific way of life changes as well as tracking down solid and pleasant ways of managing pressure helps the vast majority. I trust i've given you extraordinary ways of managing the pressure we as a whole vibe!

Most importantly, recall that you are in good company in this fight. There are countless individuals out there who feel overpowered and all the way wild. That is the reason we needed to give you this book. So you can discover a sense of harmony inside yourself and understand that we are all in this large blue marble on purpose.

You as well! Appreciate and carry on with life to its fullest. What's more, when you feel worried or hassled by a fit of anxiety, unwind, take a full breath and realize that there are many, many individuals who know precisely the way in which you feel.

The End